D0359770

Little Treasure Book

o n

WHAT WE'VE LEARNED ...SO FAR

Compiled by
H. Jackson Brown, Jr.

RUTLEDGE HILL PRESS
Nashville, Tennessee

Published in Nashville, Tennessee by Rutledge Hill Press, Inc., 211 Seventh Avenue North, Nashville, Tennessee 37219. Distributed in Canada by H. B. Fenn and Company, Ltd., 34 Nixon Road, Bolton, Ontario L7E 1W2. Distributed in Australia by The Five Mile Press, 22 Summit Road, Noble Park, Victoria 3174. Distributed in New Zealand by Tandem Press, 2 Rugby Road, Birkenhead, Auckland 10. Distributed in the United Kingdom by Verulam Publishing, Ltd., 152a Park Street Lane, Park Street, St. Albans, Hertfordshire AL2 2AU.

Typography by D&T/Bailey Typesetting, Inc., Nashville, Tennessee
Book design by Harriette Bateman

ISBN: 1-55853-555-1

Printed in Mexico
1 2 3 4 5 6 7 8 9 — 03 02 01 00 99 98 97

Introduction

All of us have had a great teacher at some time. Mine was Miss Mitchell. She was my first-grade teacher, and what I remember best was that she never criticized the colors I used when I drew. "That's lovely," she would say, and my little fingers would eagerly pick up a crayon to draw another purple horse. Partly because of her, I have never been reluctant to take chances.

And then there was Coach Hood who thought I could play first string even though I was twenty pounds lighter than the rest of the squad. In the first game of the season, I ran for two touchdowns. I still carry with me the newfound confidence I felt walking off the field that afternoon. Thank you, Coach Hood.

Then there is the one teacher we all share—the oldest, wisest, and most demanding. When Experience stands at the head of the class, we all pay attention. How do you make a girl go crazy? What really happens when you lick a slug? Some lessons cannot be found in books.

We quickly learn that cars roll down steep driveways when the emergency brakes are released and that, nine times out of ten, a tall person will sit in front of a short one at the movies. But sometimes hope triumphs over experience—for there are a few of us who, regardless of how many times we've been disappointed by the picture on the box, still buy the cereal with the toy inside.

—H. Jackson Brown, Jr.

A special thank you to those children whose artwork was submitted for this book including Julie Andress, Nicholas Castle, Scott Caven, Anika Dharamrup, Carolyn Long, Jane Mosbacher, Sara Pilzer, Brad Reinhardt, Navit Robkin, Stuart Shapiro, Amanda Taggart, and Courtney Wrenn.

Have a friend that you can confide in. It's better than a million dollars.

— *Rachel, Age 12*

You shouldn't eat Oreo cookies while wearing braces.

— *Heather, Age 13*

Never smart off to a teacher
whose eyes and ears are
twitching.
— *Andrew, Age 9*

■ ■ ■

When you jump down
stairs, take your hands out of
your pockets.
— *Philip, Age 11*

Don't mess with a kid that
beat you up once already.

— *Donnie, Age 10*

Remember that when a girl
keeps on teasing you and says
she doesn't like you and bugs
you all the time, she really
likes you.

— *Justin, Age 8*

10

Popping popcorn without a lid isn't smart.

— Alex, Age 11

When you are really stressed out, the cure is to put two miniature marshmallows up your nose and try to "snort" them out.

— *Meredith, Age 11*

■ ■ ■

No matter how hard you try, you can't baptize cats!

— *Laura, Age 13*

If a teacher is absent, when she comes back, act like you missed her.

— *Chris, Age 12*

At camp, never jump off your top bunk and expect to fly.

— *Becky, Age 8*

You should never turn on a dustbuster and hold a cat at the same time.

— *Jennifer, Age 15*

14

Never mention ice cream while you're baby-sitting if you're not sure there's some in the refrigerator.

— *Michelle, Age 11*

■ ■ ■

Don't ever try anything you've seen on *Beavis and Butthead*.

— *Danny, Age 12*

16

Never tell your mom her diet
isn't working.

Joey, Age 10

■ ■ ■

I know there are angels
around me protecting me, but
sometimes I feel as if they're
off duty.

— Mindy, Age 12

Never pull off
the emergency
brake in a car on a
steep driveway.

— Jeremy, Age 12

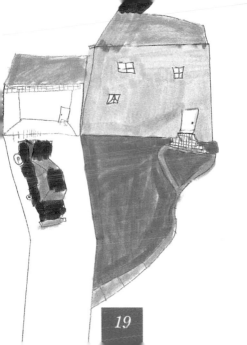

To get me up
in the morning,
the garbage
truck works
better than my
alarm clock.

— Jessica, Age 10

Don't eat food after you dissect something in science class. You just might get sick.
— *Julie, Age 12*

■ ■ ■

Remember that whining doesn't solve problems.
— *Melissa, Age 10*

Even if you are short,
stand tall because someone
looks up to you.

— *Lauren, Age 12*

■ ■ ■

Never try to hide a piece of
broccoli in a glass of milk.

— *Rosemary, Age 7*

24

Never
jump out of a
tree using
trash bags as
parachutes.

— April, Age 10

Never run around a barn with
bare feet.

— *Abbie, Age 15*

Remember that giving doesn't
count if you don't want what
you're giving away.

— *Lois, Age 11*

Don't expect the tooth fairy
to always come. Sometimes
she's broke.
— *Jeffrey, Age 8*

■ ■ ■

If you want to get even with
someone at camp, rub their
underwear in poison ivy.
— *Mark, Age 11*

When you put a hot dog in
the microwave for five
minutes, you don't want to be
there when your mom sees the
mess.

— *Jack, Age 12*

■ ■ ■

Learning to forgive
takes practice.

— *Anne, Age 14*

Always try, even when you don't think it will help.

— *Jennifer, Age 11*

When you're wearing suspenders with one strap down, be careful when going to the bathroom.

— *Nathan, Age 10*

Don't make
the mistake of
opening an
umbrella in
the car.

— Ryan, Age 7

If you are going to mix different ingredients in a mixer, don't turn it on high.

— *Victoria Emma Rose, Age 12*

■ ■ ■

Never eat a Butterfinger in front of a hungry dog.

— *Charlie, Age 11*

It's not a good idea to call 911
when there is not an
emergency.

— *Corey, Age 7*

■ ■ ■

Never ask women their
weight or age.

— *Dan, Age 12*

Sometimes you should
shut your mouth and
open your mind.
— *Chris, Age 10*

■ ■ ■

Listen to your brain.
It has lots of information.
— *Chelsea, Age 7*

If you believe in yourself,
anything is possible.
— *Meghann, Age 13*

Never let your wildest,
craziest friend put her hand on
the back of your head in front
of a whipped cream cake.
— *Katherine, Age 8*

36

Try not
to sneeze when
someone is cutting
your hair.

— *Adrienne, Age 12*

When you get a baby out of the tub, put a diaper on it immediately.

— *Jamie, Age 13*

■ ■ ■

I should always try my best. If I don't succeed, then at least I will feel good about myself.

— *Laura, Age 16*

Read lots of books. They can take you to places you haven't been before.

— *Lindsay Ellen, Age 10*

■ ■ ■

Remember, there's always room for dessert.

— *Kelly, Age 10*

You can't
catch
a hard
baseball
in your
mouth.

— Joseph, Age 10

Never wear your swimsuit on
a two-hour ride in the car.

— *Katie, Age 9*

Don't be discouraged if
you're not always perfect
on the first try.

— *Jenna, Age 10*

When you want to cheer up yourself, try cheering up someone else.

— *Heather, Age 12*

If I could learn from all my mistakes, I'd be a genius.

— *Connie, Age 13*

44

I sometimes get a craving for chocolate chip ice cream that cannot be controlled.

— *Rebecca, Age 11*

Never stick a hanger in a light socket.

— ConiRose, Age 10

Never spit while on a roller coaster.

— Scott, Age 11

Before you go to the dentist,
brush your teeth.

— Kate, Age 11

Even if someone dares you,
don't stick your tongue to a car
bumper in freezing weather.

— Tamara, Age 13

Say your prayers every night.
— *Diana, Age 9*

■ ■ ■

It's important to forgive
everyone, even people on
airplanes who have screaming
babies or who kick the back of
your seat.
— *Keera, Age 12*

When you lick a slug, your tongue goes numb.

— *Bethany, Age 11*

If you sleep in your clothes, you won't have to get dressed in the morning.

— *Stephanie, Age 8½*

You should
not be the first
one to fall
alseep at a
slumber party.

— Katie, Age 12

Never chew on an opened
tube of crazy glue.
— *Teri, Age 13*

When you go somewhere
and they say,
"Don't bring valuables,"
DON'T BRING VALUABLES.
— *Chalonne, Age 12*

Don't agitate your big sister
when she's having a
bad hair day.
— *Jimmy, Age 14*

■ ■ ■

Don't be surprised if you gain
five pounds on the scale at the
doctor's office.
— *Kathleen, Age 12*

The color of people

shouldn't matter.

— Somer, Age 10

You should never get involved in a good TV show while cooking something in the microwave.

— *Scott, Age 12*

Don't do pranks at a police station.

— *Sam, Age 10*

Always wear a hat when
feeding sea gulls.
— *Rocky, Age 9*

■ ■ ■

Being popular doesn't make
you happy, but being happy
makes you popular.
— *Jaclyn, Age 12*

You can't hide mashed potatoes in your hat.

— *Chris, Age 9*

The only time you're
guaranteed not to get
something you want is when
you don't try for it.

— *Joseph, Age 13*

■ ■ ■

Stay away from prunes.

— *Randy, Age 9*

Don't give your dog a bath unless you want to get one yourself

— Mindy, Age 14

■ ■ ■

Never leave a seven-year-old with a bat and ball alone by a window while baby-sitting him.

— Sara, Age 13

61

It's always easier to *stay* out of trouble than to *get* out of trouble.

— *Gilbert, Age 10*

■ ■

Don't wear polka-dot underwear under white shorts.

— *Jama Lynne, Age 15*

Don't use liquid soap in a
dishwasher.

— *Melinda, Age 13*

Every time you get a good
seat at the movies,
someone taller comes and
sits in front of you.

— *Kari, Age 15*

You should
never sneeze with
a chewed-up nut in
your mouth.
It's a nasty
experience.

— *Amanda, Age 14*

You shouldn't try to test a
nine-volt battery with your
braces unless you're looking
for an easy way to melt all the
rubber bands.

— *Chris, Age 14*

■ ■ ■

Never drink anything while
hanging upside down.

— *Misty, Age 12*

66

To make a girl go crazy, put a June bug down her dress.

— *Arnold, Age 6*

■ ■ ■

Never stand in a bucket of water and touch an electric fence just because your brother tells you to.

— *Melissa, Age 13*

At school,
don't mess with
the principal.

— Nicholas, Age 9

69

You should never order
seafood at a hamburger joint
in Nebraska.
— *Chad, Age 11*

■ ■ ■

It's OK to fail, but it is not OK
to give up.
— *Kate, Age 8*

You can do things that get
you in trouble, but sometimes
it's worth it.

— *Jack, Age 8*

■ ■ ■

Beware of cafeteria food when
it looks like it's moving.

— *Rob, Age 10*

72

If you're bored,
try slurping a
Slurpee® through
your nose.

-- Holly, Age 12

When you want to stay home
from school, you have to stay
in the bathroom a long,
long time.

— *Joseph, Age 11*

■ ■ ■

Never try to climb a pine tree
with shorts on.

— *Leslie, Age 11*

Pray for your enemies instead of fighting with them. It will help both them and you.

— Misty, Age 11

■ ■ ■

Never put a marshmallow in the microwave.

— Mary, Age 12

You never, ever, ever go to bed with gum in your mouth.

— *Erin, Age 13*

Never put a live bullet into the campfire.

— *Mitch, Age 13*

Once you put your quarter in the machine and turn the knob, you realize the quarter was better than the thing you got.

— *Natalie, Age 9*

Sometimes you take too much food at dinner and you can't eat it. Always make sure you have a baked potato because you can eat the middle and use the skin to hide the food until you take it to the sink. Then shove it down the disposal.

— *Chris, Age 14*

Never tease a goose.

— *Robbie, Age 12*

Never ride
your bike in mud
when you don't
know how
deep it is.

— *Corey, Age 12*

Never surprise a cow when you're standing behind her.

— Lynn, Age 12

Always carve your initials in the peanut butter when you open a new jar.

— Matt, Age 10

To make a new friend,
sometimes you have to make
the first move.

-- *Pamela, Age 10*

Putting your vegetables on
your little sister's plate
doesn't work.

— *Nicole, Age 11*

84

You should never wear a red shirt with black polka dots because your friends will call you a lady bug.

— *Stefanie, Age 8*

Never fall in love at summer camp.

— *Elizabeth, Age 11*

Maybe being a grownup will be hard, but getting there is a lot harder.

— *Chelsea, Age 14*

You shouldn't try to do fifteen
cartwheels in a row.

— *Vanessa, Age 10*

Remember, if you make a
mistake, it's not the
end of the world.

— *Marisa, Age 12*

If you put a frog in a girl's desk, you're going to hear some screaming.

— *Nicholas, Age 9*

Be careful around those younger than you. It is surprising how much of an impact a word or action can make on them.

— *Sarah, Age 12*

■ ■ ■

Never get attached to a puppy you can't have.

— *Jennifer, Age 13*

You should never aggravate a
rabbit to the point where she
starts to grunt.

— Kellie May, Age 11

■ ■ ■

No matter how much you
think you need it,
don't borrow money!

— Amy, Age 12

When you're feeling down, brush your teeth. It makes you feel like a new person.

— *Stephanie, Age 14*

■ ■ ■

Remember that Santa Claus has good years and bad years.

— *Jerry, Age 10*

When a teacher is in a bad mood, don't ask to go to the bathroom.

— *Angela, Age 11*

■ ■ ■

Never baby-sit a two-year-old without kneepads or a helmet.

— *Kelly, Age 12*

The world is a
wonderful place,
and everyone
should shut up and
enjoy it every once
in a while.

— Sarah, Age 12

95